Three Little Kittens

Written by Carole Osterink
Illustrated by Kathi Ember

Three little kittens lost their mittens,
and they began to cry.

"I can't find my mittens!"
said the first little kitten.

"Mine are lost, too! What will we do?"
said the second little kitten.

"Well, we can buy new mittens!"
said the third little kitten.

5

So they went to the store.

The first kitten picked mittens with stripes.
"Very nice!"

The second kitten picked bright pink mittens.
"I like these!"

The third kitten picked fuzzy white mittens.
"These are fine mittens!"

9

"Are these your mittens, little kittens?
I found them on the sidewalk."

The kittens smiled. They said, "Thank you for being so kind."

Three little kittens found their mittens,
and they began to sigh.

"I wanted new mittens," said the first kitten.

"I don't like these mittens," said the second kitten.

13

"Well, we still have money," said the third
kitten. "We can buy some pie."

So the three little kittens went to the
bake shop.

And they each had a slice of pie.